Mental Floss™

I quote others only to better express myself.

The two most engaging powers of an author are to make new things familiar and familiar things new.

"I truly enjoyed reading <u>Mental Floss</u>. This is one of the finest collections of sayings—an excellent resource of enlightening, uplifting and inspiring wisdom for all. A precious gift for the balance of the body and mind."

Moshé Zwang, N.D., Ph.D., the discoverer of Palm Therapy™ and the author of "Palm Therapy: Program your mind through Your Palms" and "The Ultimate Prophecy"

"Thank you, Marilyn. Once again your warmth, wisdom, and willingness to share from all you've lived and learned will bring help and healing to people in need. <u>Mental Floss</u> will certainly be part of my prescription for 'emotional fitness.'"

Bonnie Goodman M.S., L.M.H.C., Clinical Psychotherapy, Author "Choices", Composer "Songs for Recovery"

"What a delightful collection of quotes to help keep the mind fresh and clean. Marilyn Gellis is a terrific "mental hygienist" and her book is a great reminder of the inspirations that others have given us. It's a book to keep close at hand."

Christopher J. McCullough, Ph.D., Therapist—Author, Founder/Director San Francisco Anxiety Phobia Recovery Center

"<u>Mental Floss</u> should be on every entrepreneur's book shelf. These are the thoughts that lead to great achievement and excellence in business."

Janet Newcomb, M.B.A., Public Relations Consultant

"Once a light is turned on, you no longer stumble in the dark. Dr. Gellis provides the switch to illuminate your life in her latest book, <u>Mental Floss</u>."

Rose Kling, Author/Artist

"Determination and perseverance personify Dr. Gellis. <u>Mental Floss</u> is another gem in her quest to help humanity. The inspirational quotations are more valuable than diamonds."

Lillian Murray, Political Activist

"<u>Mental Floss</u> is a dynamic avenue on the road to self-esteem for students, teachers and parents."

Sherry Ann Scherotter, Guidance Counselor

For years parents, relatives, teachers, counselors, friends, neighbors, clergymen, doctors, psychologists, psychiatrists, newspaper columnists, magazine articles, self-help books, radio and television call-in talk shows, etc. have tried to help you overcome negative, defeating thoughts, actions and behaviors that have immobilized, encumbered, constrained and disabled you, but now, all of the wisdom of the ages is included in one book—MENTAL FLOSS, which contains many gems of brevity—a collage of ideas focused on content rather than words, such as:

— "The brain is as strong as its weakest think."
— "Blessed are they who can laugh at themselves because they shall never cease to be amused."
— "Speak when you're angry and you'll make the best speech you'll ever regret."
— "The art of being wise is the art of knowing what to overlook."
— "The same letters are in the word 'listen' as are in 'silent'."
— "Negative thoughts are much like acid. They do more damage to the container in which they are stored than to the object on which they are poured."
— "Some people give and forgive, others get and forget."
— "Digging for facts is much better exercise than jumping to conclusions."
— "Worrying is stewing without doing."

Some books are meant to be tasted, others to be swallowed, and few to be chewed and digested—MENTAL FLOSS is such a book, and although small in size, it speaks volumes that will challenge, excite, and inspire by providing your mind with the nourishment needed for transformation and growth—redemption and rebirth, enabling you to reach your full potential and joie de vivre.

— Dr. Marilyn Gellis, Director/Founder Institute for Phobic Awareness Author of *The Twelve Steps of Phobics Anonymous* and *From Anxiety Addict to Serenity Seeker.*

Acknowledgements

We have tried to give credit where credit was due. If we have infringed upon any copyrighted materials, we apologize. It was done innocently and if you write to us, we will gladly give credit in our next edition. Parts of this text have been reproduced from "The Twelve Steps of Phobics Anonymous" and "From Anxiety Addict to Serenity Seeker," with permission from the publisher.

In no way is this book to serve as a substitute for medical treatment.

The Institute for Phobic Awareness
Phobics Anonymous World Service Headquarters
P.O. Box 1180
Palm Springs, CA 92263-1180

Phobics Anonymous, and our P.A. symbol are registered trademarks of The Institute for Phobic Awareness.

© 1996 Dr. Marilyn Gellis   ™

ISBN: 0962-7373-4-8   Library of Congress #TX 4-312-722

Introduction

This book was not written in the "conventional" manner. Rather it evolved, developed and grew slowly from the fruits of other people's genius. Many years were spent collecting and recording this assortment of quotations, axioms, witticisms, thoughts, aphorisms, proverbs, maxims, truisms, inspiring sayings, admonitions, and insightful advice which I personally used to sustain me during a major clinical depression that was the result of acute anxiety, panic attacks and agoraphobia. I eventually became completely housebound. Fear, panic, and pessimistic, negative, catastrophic thoughts flooded my mind as soon as I awoke each morning, accompanied by a pounding, racing heartbeat, sweaty palms and an immediate desperate and urgent need to escape from the terror and feelings that I was going to go crazy, lose control or die. I faced each day with agony and dread. I didn't realize that I was manufacturing my own misery by the negative manner in which I thought about life. My irrational obsession with my imaginary problems left me brain drained, dull and apathetic with no will to live and no time or energy to seek a solution. The only light I saw at the end of the tunnel was an oncoming train.

One day in the midst of my doom and gloom while sitting on my "pity pot" I remembered my mother telling me that "The happiness of your life depends on the quality of your thoughts" and thus started my journey to courage, confidence and wellness. I began collecting positive sayings, cliches, homilies, marking books, copying passages on scraps of paper, highlighting articles, ripping out bits and pieces of newspapers, magazines and pamphlets, cutting up calendars, reading bumper stickers and posters, saving the sayings in fortune cookies, etc., etc., etc. Some wound up posted on my refrigerator, bathroom mirror, kitchen bulletin board, under glass on my desk, on my classroom walls, on the car dashboard and any other place there was an empty space.

Slowly, one day at a time, I found that by altering my thought processes I was altering my life. Ridding my mind of anything negative allowed me to evict the darkness and demons that I allowed to live there rent free.

This book is my way of sharing with you part of my collection, with the hope that you will find the contents inspiring, insightful, wise and helpful. It is meant to change, challenge, enrich and influence the way you see yourself and the world, thereby making your daily living the joyful, rewarding, fulfilling experience that life should be.

There is no specific order. Nothing is arranged according to categories, problems or relative importance. Many of the original sources are unknown to me but I think the authors in their great wisdom would rather have you pay attention to what was said than who said it.

As you read this book remember you are not merely trying to acquire information but are attempting to form new thought processes. Through time, persistence and daily application you will notice that character flaws can be replaced by positive qualities.

Mental Floss was contemplated and compiled based upon the concept that every day we all perform a series of rituals designed to promote good physical health: we bathe, eat, exercise, take vitamins, visit our doctors, etc. But how many of us get a mental check-up from the neck up?

For good dental health, we visit our dentist at least twice a year. He tells us to nourish our bodies by eating the correct foods and to always brush and floss after every meal to stimulate the gums and remove the debris that, if allowed to remain in our teeth, cause infection, decay, and possible bone loss.

In similar fashion, I believe that we should allow time and planned efforts to maintain our Mental Health.

Our minds are unique and flexible—always thinking, learning, knowing, remembering, expanding, imagining, creating, growing, discovering, awakening, integrating, absorbing, storing, evaluating, processing and discarding information and we alone are in control of the direction our minds take. Thus, it is by choice, either conscious or unconscious that we dwell on negative outcomes rather than positive projections.

Changing partners, jobs, cities, or countries cannot change who and what we are. The change only comes from within, from deep searching, redirection and revitalization of our thoughts, attitudes, values, and behaviors —

WE ARE WHAT WE THINK!

Directions for Use

Floss a minimum of three times daily and again when you find any negativity entering your mind. You will experience fast, effective relief of sensitive nerves by stimulating, massaging, polishing and promoting the healing ingredients for mental hygiene.

Mental Floss will enable you to rid your brain of the debris, disease and decay caused by stinkin' thinkin' that presently exists in the deepest cavities, crevices, nooks, crannies, and recesses of your mind, keeping you emotionally shackled.

Drain the abscess. Then extract the roots of pain and misery formulated in your early years and compounded by a lifetime of drilling self-defeating, pessimistic, negative, catastrophic thoughts and attitudes into your subconscious that you have unsuccessfully tried to anesthetize with alcohol, drugs, food, work, sex and other addictive behaviors.

By persistent mental flossing and determination you can unlock your potential, filling the void in your life with dignity, wholeness, serenity, understanding, courage, focus, balance and acceptance. The joy, zest, and thrill of living will return.

Mental Floss will enable you to experience an amazing improvement within yourself, allowing you to assume control over your circumstances rather than continuing to be directed by them. Your positive new belief system will encourage an optimistic, positive attitude.

After the final rinse, the end result will be a happy, healthy mind and a radiant, contagious smile!

"Success or failure is caused more by
mental attitude than by mental capacity."
Sir Walter Scott

"Men are not worried about things,
but by their idea of things.
When we meet difficulties,
we become anxious or troubled.
Let us not blame others but rather ourselves.
That is: our idea about things."
Epictetus

"Imagination is more important than information"
Albert Einstein

"The greater part of our happiness or misery
depends on our dispositions and not our circumstances."
Martha Washington

"We are as happy as we make up our minds
that we are going to be."
Abraham Lincoln

"Where observation is concerned,
Chance favors only the prepared mind."
Louis Pasteur

"The mind is its own place and in itself
it can make heaven of hell, or hell of heaven."
Milton

"If thou are pained by any external thing, it is not this
thing that disturbs thee but thy own judgement about it.
And, it is in thy power to wipe out this judgement now."
Marcus Aurelius

"A man's life is what his thoughts make of it."
Marcus Aurelius

"Do not think that what is hard for thee to master
is impossible for man,
but if a thing is possible and proper to man,
deem it attainable by thee."
Marcus Aurelius

"The highest possible stage in moral culture is when we
recognize that we ought to control our thoughts."
Charles Darwin

"Most of the time we think we're sick,
it's all in the mind."
Thomas Wolfe

"They conquer who believe they can."
Ralph Waldo Emerson

"A man is what he thinks about all day long."
Ralph Waldo Emerson

"Beware of an idea whose time has come."
Ralph Waldo Emerson

"Great men are those who see that thoughts rule the world."
Ralph Waldo Emerson

"Attitudes are more important than facts."
Dr. Karl Menninger

"Nothing is either good or bad, it's thinking that makes it so."
Shakespeare

"Our belief at the beginning of a doubtful undertaking is the one thing that insures the successful outcome of our venture."
William James

"The greatest discovery of my generation is that human beings can alter their lives by altering their attitude and mind."
William James

"Nurture your mind with great thoughts.
To believe in the heroic makes heroes."
Benjamin Disraeli

"Every good thought you think is contributing its share to
the ultimate result of your life."
Grenville Kleiser

"I saw that all the things I feared and which feared me
had nothing good or bad in them save insofar as the mind
was affected by them."
Spinoza

"Imagination is stronger than knowledge.
Dreams are more powerful than facts.
Hope always triumphs over experience.
Laughter is the only cure for grief,
and love is stronger than death."
Robert Fulghum

"I learned to seek my happiness by limiting my desires
rather than attempting to satisfy them."
John Stewart Mill

"Rule your mind or it will rule you."
Horace

"My life is one long obstacle course
with me as the chief obstacle."
Jack Paar

"Take charge of your attitude. Don't let someone else
change it for you. Never underestimate your power to
change yourself. Become the most positive and enthusias-
tic person you know."
H. Jackson Brown Jr.

"Conditions are created by thoughts far more powerful
than conditions create thoughts. Feelings of confidence
depend upon the type of thoughts that habitually occupy
your mind."
Norman Vincent Peale

"Always aim at complete harmony of thought and word and
deed. Always aim at purifying your thoughts and everything
will be well. There's nothing more potent than thought;
deed follows word and word follows thought. The word is
the result of a mighty thought, and where the thought is
mighty and pure the result is always mighty and pure."
Mohandas K. Gandhi

"Any idea seriously entertained tends to bring
about the realization of itself."
Joseph Chilton Pearce

"Awake or asleep man thinks. Sometimes it seems as though the chief distinction between powerful and effective men lay in the control and direction of their thoughts; the wise and energetic mind contrives to use his mind even while his body sleeps; the stupid helpless man dreams half of his life away even when his eyes are open."
Gilbert Highnet

"The human mind is capable of far more work than it has ever done. A normal man uses nearly all of his muscles during his mature life but leaves large areas, perhaps two thirds of his brain dormant. Day and night from childhood to old age, sick or well, asleep or awake, men and women think; the brain works like a heart ceaselessly pulsing. In its three pounds weight of tissue are recorded and stored billions upon billions of memories, habits, instincts, abilities, desires, and hopes and fears, patterns and tinctures and sounds, and inconceivably delicate calculations and brutishly crude urgencies."
Gilbert Highnet

"I am the master of my fate, and the captain of my soul."
William Henley

"I have the ability to redirect and regulate my thinking and to establish order and power in my emotions."
Anonymous

"We fear not only in our minds but in our hearts, brains and viscera, that whatever the cause of fear and worry, the effects can always be noted in the cells, tissues and organs of the body."

Dr. George Crile

"Emotions and feelings are quite as real as germs and no less respectable. The resultant pain and suffering of diseases caused by the emotions are no more imaginary than those caused by bacteria."

Dr. Edward Weiss

"Fundamental progress has to do with the reinterpretation of basic ideas."

Alfred North Whitehead

"Better keep yourself clean and bright. You are the window through which you must see the world."

George Bernard Shaw

"I have seen flowers come in stony places, and kindness done by men with ugly faces. And the gold cup won by the worst horse at the races, So I trust too."

John Mansefield

"Even a thought, even a possibility
can shatter and transform us."
Nietzsche

"A central feature of the theory of cognitive therapy is
that the content of a person's thinking affects his mood. A
number of studies show that inducing a subject to focus
on ideas of self-enhancing or self-deflating content produces feelings of elation or sadness, respectively."
Dr. Aaron T. Beck

"The prisoner who had lost faith in the future—his
future—was doomed. With his loss of belief in the future,
he also lost his spiritual hold; he let himself decline and
became subject to mental and physical decay.
Those who know how close the connection is between the
state of mind of a man—his courage and hope, or lack of
them—and the state of immunity of his body will understand that the sudden loss of hope and courage can have a
deadly effect."
Victor E. Frankl

"What a man is, is the basis of what he dreams and
thinks, accepts and rejects, feels and perceives."

John Mason Brown

"Nothing splendid has ever been achieved except by those who dared believe that something inside them was superior to circumstances."

Bruce Barton

"Man is what he believes."

Anton Checkhov

"All of our knowledge has its origins in our perceptions."

Leonardo da Vinci

"Life is short, art long, opportunity fleeting, experience treacherous, judgement difficult.

Hippocrates

"Our deepest fear is not that we are inadequate.
Our deepest fear is that we are powerful beyond measure.
It is our light, not our darkness, that most frightens us.
We ask ourselves, who am I to be brilliant,
gorgeous, talented and fabulous?
Actually, who are you not to be?"

Nelson Mandela,
1994 Inaugural Speech

"The people who look the most beautiful are the same as we. The only difference is they're telling themselves they look good and are letting themselves shine through.
The people who say the most profound, intelligent, or witty things are the same as we. They're letting go, being who they are.
The people who appear the most confident and relaxed are no different than we. They've pushed themselves through fearful situations and told themselves they could make it.
The people who are successful are the same as we. They've gone ahead and developed their gifts and talents and set goals for themselves. We're even the same as the people on television or in the movies: our heroes, our ideals. We're all working with approximately the same material — HUMANITY. It's how we feel about ourselves that makes the difference. It's what we tell ourselves that makes the difference."

Some people with great virtues are disagreeable, while others with great vices are delightful.

The discontented man finds no easy chair.

Yesterday's the past, tomorrow's the future,
    Today is a gift, That's why it's the "present."

        What is Life?
        Life is a challenge...meet it.
        Life is a gift...accept it.
        Life is an adventure...dare it.
        Life is a sorrow...overcome it.
        Life is a tragedy...face it.
        Life is a duty...perform it.
        Life is a game...play it.
        Life is a song...sing it.
        Life is an opportunity...take it.
        Life is a journey...complete it.
        Life is a promise...fulfill it.
        Life is beauty...appreciate it.
        Life is a goal...achieve it.
        Life is a puzzle...solve it.

God grant me the serenity
    to accept the things I cannot change,
courage to change the things that I can
    And the wisdom to know the difference.

    The best way to escape your problem is to solve it.

Be careful of your thoughts,
For your thoughts become your words.
Be careful of your words,
For your words become your actions.
Be careful of your actions,
For your actions become your habits.
Be careful of your habits,
For your habits become your character.
Be careful of your character,
For your character becomes your destiny.

Yesterday is history and
Tomorrow is a mystery.
What was…was. What is…is.
What will be is up to me.

We move toward what we picture in our minds.

If you worry about what might be
and wonder what might have been,
you'll ignore what is.

Whatever you're willing to put up with
is exactly what you will have.

If you obey all the rules, you miss all the fun.

Life is like a grindstone
Whether it grinds man down or polishes him
depends on the stuff he's made of.

A diamond is nothing but a lump of coal under pressure.

The invincible weapon against the evils of this earth is the
caring heart and the wealth of the compassionate spirit.

Many of us die with the music still inside.

It's hard to fight an enemy
that has outposts in your head.

If we spend our time with regrets over yesterday and worries over what might happen tomorrow, we have no today
in which to live.

If you have an eye on yesterday,
and an eye on tomorrow,
you're going to be cockeyed today.

The one thing that's worse than a quitter
is the person who is afraid to begin.

It's difficult to live in the present,
ridiculous to live in the future,
and impossible to live in the past.

The greatest underdeveloped territory in the world
lies under your hat.

If you are pointing the finger at someone,
three are pointing back at you!

The lowest ebb is the turn of the tide.

A day of worry is more exhausting than a week of work.

Don't be discouraged.
It's often the last key in the bunch that opens the lock.

Failure is an event, never a person.

Don't quit five minutes before the miracle happens.

The tragedy in life doesn't lie in not reaching your goal.
The tragedy lies in having no goal to reach.

Healthy minds need healthy thoughts.

We make a living by what we earn.
We make a life by what we do for others.

Success is getting what you want.
Happiness is liking what you get.

Time spent getting even is time lost getting ahead.

I will look to the moment and miraculously
the future will take care of itself.

If I were meant to live in the future,
my mind would have telescopic lenses.

Let our advance worrying become
advance thinking and planning.

If it ain't broke, don't fix it.

Expect the unexpected.

I'm so far behind, I think I'm first!

If you can't stand the heat, get out of the kitchen.

Have patience with all things, but chiefly have patience
with yourself. Do not lose courage in considering your
imperfections but start instantly remedying them. Each
day begin the task anew.

Keep on going and chances are you will
    stumble on something.
Perhaps when you are least expecting it.
I never heard of anyone stumbling on something
    sitting down.

No man is so poor as to have nothing worth giving.
    Give what you have.
To someone it may be better than you dare to think.

Do not wait for extraordinary circumstances to do good.
    Try to use ordinary situations.

Guard well within yourself that treasure, kindness.
    Know how to give without hesitation,
        how to lose without regret,
    and how to acquire without meanness.

The rat race ain't so bad if you're a big cheese.

Some minds are experts on planting and
nourishing negative feelings.
The more you think about them, the stronger they get.
Name them, claim them, then dump them.

Age is something that doesn't matter unless you are a cheese.

The only thing that makes life possible is permanent,
intolerable uncertainty; not knowing what comes next.

Man makes plans and God laughs.

When your dreams turn to dust, vacuum.

Life is not a matter of holding good cards.
It's playing a poor hand well.

Don't compromise yourself—you're all you've got.

Hope is a feeling you have
that the feeling you have isn't permanent.

The soul would have no rainbows if the eyes had no tears.

If the eyes can't weep, the organs will.

He who goes around in circles is called a big wheel.

What you have become is the price you paid
to get what you used to want.

It's not what you're eating, it's what's eating you.

Habit is habit and not to be flung out the window by any
man but to be coaxed downstairs a step at a time.

Negative thoughts are much like acid. They do more
damage to the container in which they are stored than to
the object on which they are poured.

One never notices what has been done;
one can only see what remains to be done.

It's in my power to make today a good one
just by the way I think about it and what I do about it.

Think about assets instead of liabilities.
Victories instead of defeat.

Light tomorrow with today.

Choice, not chance, determines destiny.

In youth we learn—in age we understand.

Half the truth is often a great lie.

Love and time are the only two things in all the world and
in all of life that cannot be bought, but only spent.

Never try to put an old head on young shoulders.

You may be disappointed if you fail,
but you're doomed if you don't try.

If you have made mistakes, there is always another
chance for you. You may have a fresh start any moment
you choose, for this thing we call failure is not the falling
down, but the staying down.

Today is the first day of the rest of your life.

Meditation is a mind cleaner.
Only an open, uncluttered mind can be healed.

If I lock out more than I lock in, what am I protecting?

We are each a product of our past.
We have been programmed into mindsets and attitudes
we never thought to question. We can alter our attitudes
and begin to think positively and constructively.

Reality is something you rise above.

Mistakes are part of the dues one pays for a full life.

Resolve to be thyself and know that
he who finds himself loses his misery.

Let him that would move the world first move himself.

If there is no wind — row.

If your head is wax, don't walk in the sun.

Persistence prevails when all else fails.

Life is what happens to you
while you're making other plans.

Our strength is often composed of
the weakness we're damned if we're going to show.

Happiness often sneaks in through an open door
you didn't know you left open.

Secrets are things we give to others to keep for us.

Getting what you want starts with knowing who you are.

No matter what you undertake,
you will never do it until you think you can.

The greatest power that a person possesses
is the power to choose.

All dreams come true
if we have the courage to pursue them.

A mind once stretched by a new idea
never regains its original dimensions.

Today's dream is the threshold of tomorrow's discovery.
Don't give up on the future.

A man cannot be comfortable without his own approval.

Behind peaceful tranquility lies conquered challenges.

I don't know the key to success, but the key to failure
is trying to please everybody.

It would be nice if we could forget our troubles as quickly
as we forget our blessings.

The gap between advice and help is very wide.

Think you can, or think you can't.
Either way you'll be right.

It's not the man of great native talent who wins,
but he who pushes his talent however small
to its utmost capacity.

To make the world a friendly place,
one must show a friendly face.

When love and skill work together, expect a masterpiece.

Failure is not final.

A life spent making mistakes is not only more honorable,
but more useful than a life spent doing nothing.

Everything comes to him who waits,
if he works while he waits.

Some minds are like concrete;
thoroughly mixed and permanently set.

To belittle is to be little.

The test of good manners is to put up with bad ones.

Small minds talk about people.
Average minds talk about events.
Great minds talk about concepts.

When the tide turns against you
and the current upsets your boat,
don't waste tears on what might have been.
Just lie on your back and float.

There's a natural law that says you never get something
without giving something up.

There's no such thing as a free lunch.

The clock provides only a technical measurement of how
long we live. Far more real than the ticking of time is the
way we open up the minutes and invest them with meaning.

He who marries for money usually earns it.

Borrowing trouble from the future
does not deplete the supply.

A mind set free of negatives produces positives.

If you lie down with dogs, you'll get up with fleas.

Money is a good servant, but a poor master.

He is only exempt from failure, who makes no efforts.

A strength carried to excess becomes a weakness.

All things in moderation.

It's always darkest before the dawn.

"I am like that" doesn't help anything.
"I can be different" does.

The man who believes he can do something is probably
right, and so is the man who believes he cannot.

Don't be afraid to ask dumb questions.
They're easier to handle than dumb mistakes.

If your way is dark and gloomy,
and your future is black as night,
wait—it may be a tunnel
that's a shortcut to the light.

Use whatever talents you possess.
The woods would be very silent if no birds sang
except those that sang best.

If I could buy you for what you think you're worth,
and sell you for what you're really worth,
I'd make a fortune.

If your lips would keep from slips,
five things observe with care:
to whom you speak, of whom you speak,
and how and when and where.

If you want to be respected you must respect yourself.

If you really put a small value on yourself,
rest assured that the world will not raise your price.

Think like a man of action, act like a man of thought.

Success often brings scrutiny.

Begin with the end in mind.

Seek first to understand, then to be understood.

You can't build a reputation on what you are going to do.

Time is the only coin of your life. It is the only coin you
have and only you can determine how it will be spent. Be
careful lest you let other people spend it for you.

If you trap a moment before it's ripe,
the tears of repentance you'll certainly wipe.
But if you let the right moment go,
you can never wipe off the tears of woe.

Worry is like a treadmill.
It wears you out and gets you nowhere.

Better a little pumpkin in your hand
than a big one in the field.

A bird in the hand is worth two in the bush.

Insanity is doing the same things over and over again
and expecting a different end.

This too shall pass.

If you keep doing what you're doing,
you'll keep getting what you're getting.

Never read the same book twice
since you know what the ending will be.

If your mind can conceive it, and you really believe it,
you can achieve it.

When you add to the truth, you subtract from it.

Sometimes the truth hurts like a thorn at first
but in the end it blossoms like a rose.

The heart sees better than the eye.

The greatest mistake a man can make
is to be afraid of making one.

Failure is success if we learn from it.

A man without purpose is like a ship without a rudder.

If you don't know what direction to take,
you haven't acknowledged where you are.

For the resolute and the determined
there is time and opportunity.

You can't afford the luxury of a negative thought.

No matter what may be your lot in life,
build something on it.

Obstacles are things you see
when you take your eyes off the goal.

If not now—when? If not me—who?

We are best to ourselves when we are good to others.

The secret of successful living is giving.

Reflect on your present blessings
of which every man has many.
Not on your past misfortunes,
which all men have some.

You can't turn back the clock, but you can wind it up again.

Make it a rule of life never to regret and never to look back.
Regret is an appalling waste of energy. You can't build on
it—it's only good for wallowing in.

There is not a crime, there is not a vice which does not live
in secrecy. Get these things out in the open, describe them,
attack them, ridicule them, and sooner or later, public
opinion will sweep them away.

We're as sick as our secrets.

The difficulties of life
are intended to make us better—not bitter.

Let us run with patience the race that is set before us.

In our darkest hour we might have discovered
our brightest moment.

If you trim yourself to fit the world
you'll whittle yourself away.

You can't do much about the length of your life, but you
can do something about its width and depth.

Forget injuries, never forget kindnesses.

Negative thinking is mental malpractice.

Never mind who you praise,
but be very careful whom you blame.

It it far better to follow well than to lead indifferently.

Fear not that thy life shall come to an end but fear rather
that it should never have a beginning.

Be careful what you wish for, you're liable to get it.

Flowers never emit so sweet and strong a fragrance
as before a storm.

Behold the turtle—
he makes progress only when he sticks his neck out.

Do what you feel in your heart to be right—for you'll be
criticized anyway. You'll be damned if you do and damned if
you don't.

No matter where you stand
your back is toward half the world.

Make your life a mission—not an intermission.

Living well is the best revenge.

It's better to wear out than to rust out.

The best cure for worry, depression, melancholy and
brooding is to go deliberately forth and try to lift with one's
sympathy the gloom of someone else.

Never bear more than one trouble at a time. Some people
bear three kinds: all they have had, all they now have, and
all they expect to have.

It isn't worth spending $1000 worth of emotion
on a five cent irritation.

Waste not fresh tears on old griefs.

Don't sweat the small stuff and it's all small stuff.

Resentments are rubbish—haul them away.

Clouds have linings, problems have endings.

Nothing is a problem unless we make it one.

Not everything that is faced can be changed,
but nothing can be changed until it is faced.

Have patience—in time, grass becomes milk.

It isn't the load that weighs us down, it's the way we carry it.

Life is 10% what you make it and 90% how you take it.

The difference between stumbling blocks and
stepping stones is the way man uses them.

The more difficult the obstacle,
the stronger one becomes after hurdling it.

No difficulties, no discovery, no pains, no gains.

An admission of error is a sign of strength
rather than a confession of weakness.

We are all manufacturers, making goods, making trouble,
or making excuses.

You can preach a better sermon with your life
than with your lips.

The highest reward for man's toil is not what he gets for it
but rather what he becomes by it.

Do unto others as you would have others do unto you.
We have committed the golden rule to memory—
let us now commit it to life.

What I must do and not what people think
is all that concerns me.

A man is rich according to what he is—
not according to what he has.

Children need models more than they need critics.

There is no better exercise for strengthening the heart
than reaching down and lifting people up.

What lies behind us and what lies before us are tiny matters compared to what lies within us.

There is no right way to do the wrong thing.

All that is necessary for the triumph of evil is that good men do nothing.

There isn't any map on the road to success— you have to find your own way.

Today is the tomorrow you worried about yesterday.

When you get to the end of your rope, tie a knot and hang on.

The best and most beautiful things in the world cannot be seen or touched but are felt with the heart.

Life is easier than you think. All you have to do is accept the impossible, do without the indispensable and bear the intolerable.

95% of the things that we worry about never happen.

Don't tell me that worry doesn't do any good—I know better. The things I worry about never happen.

Why is it opportunities always look bigger going
than coming?

Of all the troubles great and small
are those that never happened at all.

Nothing is ever all wrong.
Even a clock that has stopped running is right twice a day.

If you must doubt, doubt your doubts. Never your beliefs.

There is nothing permanent but change.

"Normal" is only a setting on the dryer.

The best way to succeed in life
is to act on the advice you give to others.

Swallowing your pride once in awhile
will never give you indigestion.

Life is like a ladder.
Every step we take is either up or down.

When success turns a person's head, he is facing failure.

There is no greater loan than a sympathetic ear.

Opinions that are well rooted should grow
and change like a healthy tree.

Investment in knowledge pays the best interest.

We see things not as they are but as we are.

The best victory is to conquer self.

Time cannot be expanded, accumulated,
mortgaged, hastened or retarded.

The state of a relationship's health is dependent upon
the health of the people involved.

Most people's hindsight is 20/20.

It is better to understand a little
than to misunderstand a lot.

Habit is a cable, we weave a thread of it every day
and at last we cannot break it.

I have often regretted my speech. Seldom my silence.

Failure is the path of least persistence.

Life is made up of sobs, sniffles, and smiles.

If your outgo exceeds your income,
then your upkeep will be your downfall.

I cannot change the direction of the wind, but I can
adjust my sails to always reach my destination.

Nothing is easier than fault finding:
no talent, no self-denial, no brains, no character
are required to set up in the grumbling business.

Happiness grows at our own firesides,
and is not to be picked in a stranger's garden.

A cynic is one who knows the price of everything
and the value of nothing.

It's good to have money and the things money can buy
but it's good too to check up once in a while to make sure
you haven't lost the things money can't buy.

Great minds have purposes, others have wishes.
Little minds are tamed and subdued by misfortune;
but great minds rise above them.

Today is yesterday's pupil.

Patience is bitter but its fruit is sweet.

Every man is a volume if you know how to read him.

The only place success comes before work
is in the dictionary.

Don't part with your illusions — when they are gone,
you may still exist but you have ceased to live.

To believe with certainty we must begin by doubting.

Sometimes less is more.

Expect nothing, appreciate everything, and
you'll never be disappointed.

A clean conscience is a soft pillow.

Habit is a man's best friend or his worst enemy.

A fellow who worries about what people think of him
wouldn't worry so much if he only knew how seldom
they do.

A good memory is fine but the ability to forget
is the true test of greatness.

The mind's direction is more important than its progress.

Nothing improves our prayer faster than big trouble.

There are no atheists in foxholes.

Stickability is 95% of ability.

Saints are sinners who kept on trying.

Church is not a hotel for saints but
rather a hospital for sinners.

Our problem isn't knowing what is right,
it is doing it.

People are lonely because they build walls
instead of bridges.

What happens around us is largely outside our control,
but the way we choose to react is inside our control.

Nobody does anything to you—you do it to yourself.

Idle minds are the devil's workshop.

We don't have to change our emotions consciously,
just change our thoughts and our emotions quickly follow.

Speech is the index of the mind.

Do the important, not the urgent.

It may make a difference to all eternity
whether we do right or wrong today.

The men who try to do something and fail are infinitely
better than those who try to do nothing and succeed.

A thought is an idea in transit.

The wise man hears one word but understands two.

Carry your own lantern and you need not fear the dark.

Words should be weighed, not counted.

The hardest work is being idle.

A proverb is a short sentence
based upon a long experience.

The best place to find a helping hand
is at the end of your own arm.

Four things never come back…
the spoken word, the sped arrow,
the past life and the neglected opportunity.

If you tell the truth, you don't have to remember anything.

A liar must have a good memory.

You cannot do a kindness too soon
because you never know how soon will be too late.

People who aren't afraid to roll up their sleeves
seldom lose their shirts.

We have two ears and one mouth,
that we may listen more and talk less.

Ideas are funny little things.
They don't work unless you do.

In the middle of difficulty lies opportunity.

Muddy waters let stand become clear.

No one can make you unhappy without your consent.

To mean well is nothing without to do well.

If you want work well done, select a busy man.
The other kind has no time.

The worst tempered people I've ever met
were the people who knew they were wrong.

It seems our destiny never to love anything
without seeking to alter it, and in altering it
to make it other than what we first loved.

There is a past which is gone forever;
but there is a future which is still our own.

Grief is the agony of an instant.
The indulgence of grief, the blunder of a lifetime.

Friendships will last if they are put first.

Those who bring sunshine into the lives of others
cannot keep it from themselves.

Kind words can be short and sweet,
but their echoes are truly endless.

When hands reach out in friendship,
hearts are touched with joy.

When we feel someone else's pain, we can help to lessen it.

Unshared joy is an unlighted candle.

The ornaments of a house are the friends who frequent it.

Empathy is your pain in my heart.

Don't walk in front of me, I may not follow.
Don't walk behind me, I may not lead.
Walk beside me and just be my friend.

Together we stick, divided we're stuck.

A true friend will see you through
when others see that you are through.

Some people make the world a special place
just by being in it.

Trouble is a sieve through which we sift our acquaintances.
Those too big to pass through are our friends.

A friend is a lift, not a load.
A boost, not a burden.

Snowflakes are one of nature's most fragile things, but just look at what they can do when they stick together.

A person never gets so rich
that they can afford to lose a friend.

When our load is light, it's time to carry someone else's.

A friend listens to our words but hears our heart.

We like someone because.
We love someone although.

In life, make the most of the best
and the least of the worst.

May life's greatest gifts always be yours.
Happiness, memories and dreams.

It's not only what we do, but also what we do not do
for which we are accountable.

Anger is only one letter short of danger.

Knowledge does not become power until it is used.

What sunshine is to flowers, smiles are to humanity.

It's harder to conceal ignorance
than to acquire knowledge.

The heart has its seasons but age is just a state of mind.

A gem cannot be polished without friction,
nor a man perfected without trials.

Growth depends largely upon our willingness to replace
many of our previous opinions and attitudes with a new
set of ideas.

Happiness is not the absence of conflict,
but the ability to cope with it.

Courage is resistance to fear, mastery of fear,
not absence of fear.

People who are wrapped up in themselves
make a very small package.

For fast acting relief, try slowing down.

The grand essentials to happiness in this life are:
something to do, something to love,
and something to hope for.

Anyone who limits his vision
to memories of yesterday is already dead.

It is the person who has done nothing
who is sure nothing can be done.

Time is a dressmaker specializing in alterations.

If we try too hard to force others to live in our world
because we think it's the real world, we are doomed to
disappointment.

Speak kindly today; when tomorrow comes,
you will be in practice.

If you want to make God laugh, tell him your plans.

Man proposes — God disposes.

It is far easier to stay out of trouble
than it is to get out of trouble.

You have to know the rules to know when to break them.

No one can make you feel inferior without your consent.

It's nice to be important,
but it's more important to be nice.

One faces the future with one's past.

Fear makes strangers of people who should be friends.

Limited expectations yield only limited results.

The healthy, strong individual is the one who asks for help whether he's got an abscess on his knee or in his soul.

He who angers you conquers you.

Pain is inevitable, suffering is optional.

A depressing and difficult passage has prefaced every new page I have turned in life.

The game of life is a game of boomerangs.
Our thoughts, deeds, and words return to us sooner or later with astounding accuracy.

You don't get to choose how you're going to die or when.
You can only decide how you're going to live — NOW.

Our doubts are traitors and make us lose the good we oft
might win by fearing to attempt.

A man can fail many times but he isn't a failure
until be begins to blame someone else.

What goes up always comes down.

Genius is 3% inspiration and 97% perspiration.

Tact is the ability to close your mouth
before someone else wants to.

Deal with the faults of others as gently as with your own.

We are never more discontented with others than when
we are discontented with ourselves.

If you trust, you don't worry.
If you worry, you don't trust.

Success is getting what you want.
Happiness is wanting what you get.

Each day comes bearing its gifts. Untie the ribbons.

All the flowers of all the tomorrows
are in the seeds of today.

The happiness of your life depends upon
the quality of your thoughts.

You can't get anywhere today
if you are still mired down in yesterday.

Worry is interest paid on trouble before it is due.

Through tough times always turn to the three F's:
Faith, Family and Friends.

That was then, this is now. Don't give up.

Fake it 'til you make it.

Worry gives a small thing a big shadow.

Nothing in life is to be feared.
It is only to be understood.

Luck is a matter of preparation meeting opportunity.

Friendships. The inexpressible comfort of feeling safe with a person, having neither to weigh thoughts nor measure words.

When life seems overwhelming and you feel pressured tell yourself, "I'm rough and tough and hard to bluff."

Always behave like a duck. Keep calm and unruffled on the surface, but paddle like the devil underneath.

The best way to cheer yourself up
is to try to cheer somebody else up.

Only eyes washed by tears can see clearly.

If you can't win,
make the fellow ahead of you break the record.

Why not go out on a limb?
Isn't that where the fruit is?

When a thing is done, it's done.
Don't look back, look forward to your next objective.

Always be nice to people on the way up, because you'll meet the same people on the way down.

Don't tell friends about your indigestion.
"How are you?" is a greeting, not a question.

It isn't the mountain ahead that wears you out.
It's the grain of sand in your shoe.

Enjoy present pleasures in such a way
as not to injure future ones.

Don't be afraid of opposition.
A kite rises against the wind, not with the wind.

Act — don't react!

We can't all have bright days, but one thing is true.
No cloud is so dark that the sun can't shine through.

Never grow a wishbone where your backbone should be.

Live where you stand and bloom where you are planted.

Enjoy when you can and endure when you must.

Go often to the house of a friend;
for weeds soon choke up the unused path.

Don't protect yourself with a fence,
but rather by your friends.

What you are speaks so loudly I cannot hear what you say.
Talk is cheap!

To know the road ahead, ask those coming back.

Keep your eyes on the stars and your feet on the ground.

Don't part company with your ideals,
they are anchors in a storm.

Do not be afraid of growing slowly,
be afraid of standing still.

Happiness is a way of travel, not a destination.

Let us not look back in anger or forward in fear,
but around in awareness.

It's a mistake to look too far ahead. The chain of destiny
can only be grasped one link at a time.

A chain is only as strong as its weakest link.

He who receives a benefit should never forget it.
He who bestows one should never remember it.

We must give not only what we have
but we must also give what we are.

Our attitudes are threefold.
They include beliefs, emotions, and actions.

To live a little better, always be forgiving
and add a little sunshine to the world in which we're living.

Daily living should be a rewarding
and fulfilling experience.

Progress, not perfection.

Pride halts progress.

I can only borrow trouble at high interest rates.

God is the architect. I am the builder.

If all I can see is my own shadow—I'm in my own light.

Projected fears like shadows are larger than life.

The door to the human heart can be opened
only from the inside.

Except in occasional emergencies,
there is not much that one man can do for another
other than help him help himself.

Give a man a fish, you feed him for a day.
Teach him how to fish, you feed him for a lifetime.

To handle yourself, use your head.
To handle others, use your heart.

The only safe and sure way to destroy an enemy
is to make him your friend.

Forgiveness is the fragrance the violet sheds
on the heel that crushed it.

Always forgive your enemies, nothing annoys them so much.

A friend is a present you give yourself.

Some people give and forgive, others get and forget.

It takes both rain and sunshine to make a rainbow.

The smallest good deed is better than
the grandest intention.

Do you see difficulties in every opportunity
or opportunities in every difficulty?

Plan your work, work your plan.
If you fail to plan, then plan to fail.

I can complain because rose bushes have thorns or
rejoice because thorn bushes have roses.

Some cause happiness wherever they go,
others whenever they go.

Two tragedies in life. One is not to get your heart's desire,
the other is to get it.

Praise, like gold and diamonds,
owes its value to its scarcity.

Every man's work is a portrait of himself.

If you would make a man happy, do not add to his
possessions but subtract from the sum of his desires.

The only way on earth to multiply happiness
is to divide it.

Happiness consists of activity.
It is a running stream, not a stagnant pool.

Joy is not in things, it is in us.

Gratitude is the memory of the heart.

Better to light one candle than to curse the darkness.

The secret of happy living is not to do what you like
but to like what you do.

If we pause to think, we'll have cause to thank.

Happiness is the only thing we can give without having.

With hope in our lives, all else is possible.

The secrets we keep, keep us from the health we deserve.

Readiness is the key to all important passages in life.

Try to find something that works and stay with it.

Magnificent gardens are not beautiful only because the flowers are pretty. They're beautiful because someone is controlling the weeds.

Feeling good about yourself is not a luxury; it is an absolute necessity.

That which is not written down becomes lost and vague. Success can occur in your life, but awareness is the first key.

You can always better your best and if at first you don't succeed, try another way.

When you let go of changing others and work on changing yourself, your outward conditions change.

Change occurs when we take responsibility for our own thoughts, decisions, and actions.

Your belief at the beginning of a doubtful undertaking is the one thing that insures the successful outcome of your venture.

Practice makes perfect and practice reduces fear.

Verbalize, visualize, practice and experience your fear until it no longer dominates your life.

The way you act will eventually be determined by the way you think, feel and believe.

Clarifying your values is the essential first step toward a richer, fuller, more productive life.

Yesterday is a cancelled check, tomorrow is a promissory note, today is ready cash...use it!

I challenge you to double the amount of energy and enthusiasm you are putting into your life.
I guarantee you will triple your feelings of self-esteem, happiness and success.

Finish every day and be done with it. You have done what you could. Some blunders and absurdities no doubt crept in, forget them as soon as you can.

Tomorrow is a new day; begin it well and serenely and with too high a spirit to be encumbered with your old nonsense.

This day is all that is good and fair. It is too dear, with its hopes and invitations to waste a moment on yesterday.

A positive attitude will enhance the value of every experience. The choice is up to me.

One often learns more from ten days of agony
than from ten years of contentment.

Courage is fear that has said its prayers.

I don't need to crack the code to get the message.

Every great mistake has a halfway moment, a split second
when it can be recalled and perhaps remedied.

Even welcome visitors can only enter
through a door I've opened.

If you shut the door to all errors, truth will be shut out too.

Let me not forget, my chief business in life is living.

Limited expectations yield only limited results.

To find out what I hold most precious,
I will try to imagine giving it up.

Success requires no explanations.
Failure permits no alibis.

Dreams that you dare to dream really do come true.

When you can look at yesterday without regret and
tomorrow without fear, you're on your way to living in
today.

Yesterday is ashes. Tomorrow is wood.
Only today does the fire burn brightly.

We all get two gifts we should use as much as possible.
Imagination and humor.
Imagination compensates us for what we are not.
A sense of humor consoles us for what we are.

Poor eyes limit one's sight. Poor vision limits one's deeds.

To accomplish great things, we must not only act
but also dream, not only plan, but also believe.

Habit is like a soft bed.
Easy to get into but hard to get out of.

Time wasted is existence. Time used is living.

When thoughts enter my mind uninvited,
I do my best not to let them get comfortable there.

I see the world differently by changing my mind
about what I want to see.

Worrying is stewing without doing.

Success is the journey, not the destination.

A person who aims at nothing has a target he can't miss.

The largest room in the world
is the room for improvement.

Many of our fears are paper thin and a single courageous
step would carry us clear through them.

To live well, we must have a faith fit to live by,
a self fit to live with, and a cause fit to live for.

Successful people seek a solution in every problem
rather than a problem in every solution.

Don't let life discourage you.
Everyone who got where he is had to begin where he was.

The beginnings of all things are small.
Great visions often start with small dreams.

To dream of the person you would like to be
is to waste the person you are.

The day will happen whether or not you get up.

It has been said that success
is 80% attitude and 20% aptitude.

Sorrows are like thunder clouds. In the distance they look
black, but overhead they are hardly gray.

The faults of others are like headlights on a passing car.
They seem more glaring than our own.

It takes as much energy to wish as it does to plan.

What I do today is important
because I'm exchanging a day of my life for it.

The miracle is this…the more we share, the more we have.

Life is a measure to be filled, not a cup to be drained.

It's not because things are difficult that we do not dare,
it is because we do not dare that they are difficult.

If you get some hard bumps,
at least it shows you are out of the rut.

We are not put on earth to see through one another but to see one another through.

Inch by inch life's a cinch. Yard by yard, life is hard.

Success comes in cans — not in can'ts.

Little strokes fell great oaks.

Content makes poor men rich,
discontent makes rich men poor.

Fish and visitors stink after three days.

The worst wheel of the cart makes the most noise.

Empty barrels rattle the most.

An empty bag cannot stand upright.

Well done is better than well said.

There are three things extremely hard:
steel, a diamond, and to know one's self.

If you would not be forgotten, as soon as you are dead
and rotten, either write things worth reading, or do things
worth writing.

A long life may not be good enough,
but a good life is long enough.

Men take more pains to mask than to mend.

A false friend and a shadow
attend only when the sun shines.

Be civil to all, sociable to many, familiar with few,
friend to one, enemy to none.

An open foe may prove a curse,
but a pretend friend is worse.

Wealth is not his that has it, but his that enjoys it.

He that would live in peace and at ease,
must not speak all he knows, nor judge all he sees.

Hide not your talents, they for us were made.
What's a sun dial in the shade?

If you would reap praise you must sow the seeds
of gentle words and useful deeds.

Greener pastures always have brown spots too.

Even in laughter the heart might be in pain.

Out of suffering come the strongest souls.
God's wounded often make his best soldiers.

Always wear clean underwear.
Heaven forbid you should have an accident.

God never closes one door without opening another.

Coincidence is when God works a miracle
and chooses to remain anonymous.

If at first you don't succeed try reading the directions.

You can catch more flies with honey
than you can with vinegar.

Nothing great was ever achieved without enthusiasm. It
overcomes discouragement and gets things done. It's the
magic quality, and the remarkable thing is…it's contagious!

If at first you don't succeed, you're running about average.

A good memory is fine, but the ability to
forgive and forget is the true test of greatness.

He who accepts evil without protesting it
is really cooperating with it.

You may not get what you want
but you'd better want what you get.

An admission of error is a sign of strength
rather than weakness.

Real friends are those who, when you've made a fool of
yourself, don't think you've done a permanent job.

He who seeks a friend without fault remains without one.

It doesn't matter if you're on the right track,
you'll still get run over if you don't keep moving.

Be like a postage stamp—stick to one thing
until it gets to its destination.

Face your fear and the fear will disappear.

Act in haste, repent at leisure.

It is better to suffer a wrong than to do a wrong.

The really happy man is the one who can enjoy the
scenery even when he has to take a detour.

There are only two lasting bequests we can give
our children. One is roots, the other, wings.

Go with the flow. Ride with the tide.

Our problem isn't not knowing what is right, it is doing it.

Time doesn't always heal, but it makes the hurt bearable.

An ounce of prevention is worth a pound of cure and
don't forget a stitch in time saves nine.

There are two ways of spreading light,
to be the candle or the mirror that reflects it.

The man who rows the boat
generally doesn't have time to rock it.

Haste makes waste.

If you don't get everything you want,
think of the things you didn't get that you didn't want.

If you have tried to do something and failed,
you are vastly better off than had you tried to do nothing
and succeeded.

Experience is a wonderful thing. It enables you
to recognize a mistake when you make it again.

He who has a thing to sell
and goes and whispers in a well
is not so apt to get the dollars
as he who climbs a tree and hollers.

Your lot in life depends on whether you use it
for building or for parking.

A mental concept has more voltage than electricity.
Civilizations are changed by an idea.

He who hesitates is lost.

What goes around comes around.

The thrill is not just in winning
but the courage to join the race.

As a person grows older and wiser,
he talks less and says more.

Someday there will be a banquet of consequences and
we're all going to sit down to it.

Nothing is so fatiguing as the eternal hanging on
to uncompleted tasks.

I know not what the future holds, but
I know who holds the future.

Character and ideals are catching. When you associate
with men who aspire to the highest and best, you expose
yourself to the qualities that make men great.

Fear is that little dark room where negatives are developed.

Character is not an inheritance,
each person must build it for himself.

Formula for youth—
keep your enthusiasms and forget your birthdays.

The greatness of a man is not evidenced by his
finding faults, but by fixing them.

The five most important words in the English language:
"I am proud of you."
The four most important words:
"What is your opinion?"
The three most important words:
"If you please."
The two most important words:
"Thank you."
The least important word:
"I."

Some people dream of success
while others wake up and work hard for it.

Take time to work, it is the price of success.
Take time to think, it is the source of power.
Take time to play, it is the secret of perpetual youth.
Take time to read, it is the foundation of wisdom.
Take time to be friendly, it is the road to happiness.
Take time to love and be loved, it is the privilege of the Gods.
Take time to share, life is too short to be selfish.
Take time to laugh, laughter is the music of the soul.

Today make the most of small opportunities and tasks.
They could just be the start of great things.

What good does it matter if man reaches his goal
and gains the whole world but loses his soul.
For what have we won if in gaining this end,
we've been much too busy to be kind to a friend.

After the clouds, the sunshine. After the winter, the spring.
After the shower, a rainbow. For life is a changeable thing.

Change is the only constant.

To triumph over trouble, and grow stronger with defeat,
is to win the kind of victory that will make
your life complete.

Since fear, dread, and worry cannot help in any way,
It's much healthier and happier to be cheerful every day.

The road to success is dotted with many
tempting parking places.

We learn more by welcoming criticism
than by rendering judgment.

One thing you can learn by watching the clock is that it
passes the time by keeping its hands busy.

The impossible is the untried.

No one knows the weight of another man's burden.

Holding onto grievances is a decision to suffer.

You can be part of the problem or part of the solution.

It is not so much ours to set the world right,
rather it is ours to see it rightly.

"I must do something" will always solve more problems
than "something must be done."

Forgiving uplifts the forgiver.

Man cannot discover new oceans until he has the courage
to lose sight of the shore.

Progress depends on diligence and perseverance.

Perseverance makes the difference between
success and defeat.

As within, so without.

No one knows what he can do until he tries.

Every ending is a new beginning.

We tend to find what we look for,
good or evil, problems or solutions.

Life is 10% what you make it and
90% how you take it.

It's good to have an end to journey toward,
but it's the journey that matters in the end.

Your thoughts are like boomerangs.

The seeds of destruction are sown in anger.

Expect the best, convert problems into opportunities.

Enthusiasm facilitates achievement.

Once a word has been allowed to escape,
it cannot be recalled.

Your life becomes what you think.

Worry is a rocking chair that gives you something to do,
but never gets you anywhere.

A true friend is someone who is there for you
when they would rather be anywhere else.

A happy person is not a person in a
certain set of circumstances, but rather a person
with a certain set of attitudes.

When you rule your mind, you rule the world.

There's as much risk in doing nothing
as in doing something.

Chance favors the prepared.

It's better to lead than to push.

The light of understanding dissolves the phantoms of fear.

Often a pat on the back works better
than a kick in the pants.

Defeat isn't bitter if you don't swallow it.

What we focus on expands.

Change your mind to change your life.

There is no failure except in not trying.

Minds are like parachutes—
they only function when they are open.

Never affirm self-limitations.

Defeat may test you, it need not stop you.

Without faith, nothing is possible.
With it, nothing is impossible.

People seldom see the halting and painful steps by which
the most insignificant success is achieved.

Determination and perseverance move the world;
thinking that others will do it for you is a sure way to fail.

How far you go in life depends on your being tender
with the young, compassionate with the aged,
sympathetic with the striving and tolerant of the weak
and the strong. Because someday in life you will
have been all of these.

One of the things that has helped me as much as any
other is not how long I am going to live, but how much I
could do while living.

The mind is like a volcano with two vents:
destructiveness and creativeness.

Today's preparation determines tomorrow's achievement.

Knowledge comes from taking things apart
but wisdom comes from putting things together.

Do more than exist—live.
Do more than touch—feel.
Do more than look—observe.
Do more than read—absorb.
Do more than listen—understand.

The thing to try when all else fails is again.

Nature give us two ends—one to sit on and one to think
with. Success or failure is dependent upon which one is
used most.

Do what you can with what you have, where you are.

Experience is a hard teacher because she gives the test
first, the lesson afterwards.

Youth is a gift of nature, but age is a work of art.

The word "listen" contains the same letters as the word "silent".

Digging for facts is much better exercise
than jumping to conclusions.

Experience is the one thing most of us would be glad to
sell for less than we paid for it.

Do not stare up the steps to success.
Step up the stairs.

The only thing achieved in life without effort is failure.

There is always free cheese in a mousetrap.

You have to know the ropes in order to pull the strings.

If you want to keep your feet on the ground,
put some responsibility on your shoulders.

Cooperation is spelled with two letters—WE.

If the ruts are so deep in the road that you're scraping
bottom, maybe it's time to try a different road.

Never confuse activity with productivity.

The difference between ordinary and extraordinary
is that little extra.

Master yourself and you can master anything.

Progress always involves risk:
You can't steal second base if you keep your foot on first.

The simplest things are often the hardest to grasp—
like soap in the shower.

There's no traffic jam going the extra mile.

Use soft words and hard arguments.

Life is an educational process where know-how is good;
know-when is better, and know-who is best.

Four steps to accomplishment:
Plan purposefully, prepare prayerfully,
proceed positively, and pursue persistently.

The courage to speak must be matched by
the wisdom to listen.

Be bold in what you stand for,
but cautious in what you fall for.

There are three ways to get up in this world without a lot of hard work: in an elevator or an escalator, and by using an alarm clock.

The most difficult mountains to climb are the ones we make out of molehills.

Few of us get dizzy from doing too many good turns.

We must all learn to bear and forbear, forgive and forget.

Food for the mind should be considered as carefully as food for the body.

Don't stop because you failed
or you will fail because you stopped.

It's not what you know but what you are
that determines happiness.

To move a mountain you must begin
by carrying away small stones.

Problems would lessen if people would listen.

The train of thought can take you to a better station in life.

Prepare and prevent instead of repair and repent.

Life may be full of hard knocks, but answer them all—
one might be an opportunity.

People who bite the hand that feeds them usually lick the
boot that kicks them.

The service we render others is really the rent we pay for our
room on Earth.

Every man has three characters—
that which he exhibits, that which he has, and that which he
thinks he has.

All of your problems can only be cured retail, but you can
prevent them wholesale.

Every man's memory is his private literature.

The present is the period when the future pauses for a short
while before becoming the past.

He who has a why to live can bear almost any how.

Tact is the art of making a point without making an enemy.

We think in generalities—we live in detail.

A man who dares not waste one hour of time
has not discovered the value of life.

When it's dark enough, you can see the stars.

Of all the things you wear,
your expression is the most important.

There are three great questions in life that we have to
answer over and over again: Is it right or wrong?
Is it true or false? Is it beautiful or ugly?
Only our education can help answer them.

Not he who has little but he who wishes more is poor.

To get profit without risk, experience without danger
and reward without work is as impossible as it is
to live without being born.

It is possible to own too much. A man with one watch knows
what time it is, a man with two watches is never quite sure.

Never trust anyone who doesn't have an opinion.

The way we talk about other people
tells more about us than them.

The most important lessons are the ones we teach ourselves—experience is the best teacher.

Treat people as if they were what they ought to be and you
help them to become what they are capable of being.

Pride is not found in being the best, but in doing your best.

One of the greatest labor-saving inventions of today
is tomorrow.

We are told that talent creates its own opportunities, but it
sometimes seems intense desire creates not only its own
opportunities but its own talents.

There is a mighty difference between good sound reasons
and reasons that sound good.

Riches consist not in the extent of one's possessions, but in
the fewness of one's wants.

If I have been able to see farther than others
it is because I stood on the shoulders of giants.

Men fear silence as they fear solitude because both give them a glimpse of the terror of life's nothingness.

If money is your hope for independence, you will never have it. The only real security that a man can have in this world is a reserve of knowledge, experience, and ability.

Judge a man by his questions rather than by his answers.

Stand up for what is right even if you're standing alone.

The bitterest tears shed over graves are for words left unsaid and deeds left undone.

They talk the most who have the least to say.

If you want to hit the bull's eye every time, throw the dart first and then draw circles around it.

Time wounds all heels.

Speak when you're angry and you'll make the best speech you'll ever regret.

Silence is one of the hardest things to repute.

A man begins cutting his wisdom teeth the first time
he bites off more than he can chew.

The art of being wise is the art of knowing what to overlook.

Man does not live by words alone, despite the fact that he
sometimes has to eat them.

The thoughtless are rarely wordless.

We work to become — not to acquire.

The brain is as strong as its weakest think.

Too many people are thinking security instead of
opportunity. They seem more afraid of life than death.

The impossible is often the untried.

There are two ways of exerting one's strength.
One is pushing down, the other is pulling up.

A man never discloses his own character so clearly
as when he describes another's.

The finest steel has to go through the hottest fire.

Tears are antifreeze for the soul.

Sanity is the playground for the unimaginative.

Straight trees may have crooked roots.

If you run with turkeys, don't expect to soar with eagles.

When the student is ready, the teacher will appear.

The power to punish is not as great as the power to forgive.

Dignity does not consist in possessing honors,
but in deserving them.

Hope is merely disappointment deferred.

Waiting and hoping are the whole of life and as soon as the
dream is realized, it is destroyed.

Each morning puts a man on trial and
each evening passes judgement.

Not to decide is to decide.

The time you enjoy wasting is not wasted time.

The hardest thing in life to learn is which bridge to cross
over and which to burn.

The course of life is unpredictable.
No one can write his autobiography in advance.

The tragedy of life is what dies inside a man
while he still lives.

Against logic there is no armor like ignorance.

There is only one success—
to be able to spend your life in your own way.

Life is a vast mysterious ocean of discovery,
and most of us stay on the shore,
afraid of what we'll encounter if we jump in.

True friendship is like good health:
the value of it is never known until it is lost.

One of our greatest weaknesses is our apparent inability to
distinguish our needs from our greeds.

Every man must do his own growing no matter how tall his
ancestors were.

The purpose of learning is growth, and our minds, unlike our
bodies, can continue growing as long as we live.

Happiness is the interval between periods of unhappiness.

May the most you want be the least you get and may the
happiest days of the past be the saddest days of your future.

Happy is the man who learns early in life the wide chasm
that lies between his wishes and his powers.

Hatred is like a fire: It makes even light rubbish deadly.

Some are born good, some make good,
and some are caught with the goods.

Only in forgiving are we forgiven.

Success has made failures of many men.

Man cannot remake himself without suffering,
for he is both the marble and the sculptor.

Out of suffering have emerged the strongest souls.
The most massive characters are seared with scars.

There are so many things that we wish we had done yesterday, so few that we feel like doing today.

Today is the most important thing in life. It comes unto us at
midnight very clean. It's perfect when it arrives and it puts
itself in our hands. It hopes we learned something from yesterday.

There are only two ways of getting on in this world:
by one's own industry or by the weakness of others.

I'm a great believer in luck and I find the harder I work,
the more of it I have.

Nothing is really work unless you would rather be
doing something else.

That man is richest whose pleasures are cheapest.

We don't all need someone to live with,
but rather someone to be alive with.

The only man who can change his mind
is the man who has one.

Have the courage to live — anyone can die.

The chains of habit are too weak to be felt until
they are too strong to be broken.

Destiny is not a matter of chance. It is a matter of choice.
It is not a thing to be waited for. It is a thing to be achieved.

Wise men learn by other men's mistakes. Fools by their own.

To err is human but when the eraser wears out
ahead of the pencil, you're overdoing it.

Success goes to your head, failure to your heart.

There are two kinds of failures — those who thought and
never did, and those who did and never thought.

There are three kinds of friends:
best friends, guest friends, and pest friends.

The price of greatness is responsibility.

We can choose to throw stones, to stumble on them,
or to climb over them and build with them.

The joy of yesterday can be found in the memory of today.

It's the difference that makes the difference.

It's better to know a little about something
than a lot about nothing.

Jack of all trades, master of none.

No good deeds ever go unpunished.

A little knowledge is a dangerous thing.

Put a beggar on horseback,
he'll ride you to death.

Words are easy to spill, but hard to clean up.

Despair and depression must not be allowed to have
unchallenged dominance in our minds for they become habit
patterns of the most constricting kind.

The day will come when the risk to be closed in a bud will
become more painful than the risk it takes to blossom.

It's not what you say that's important, it's what they hear.

When we stop becoming part of life's problems we begin to
become part of its answers.

Negative thoughts are breeding grounds for disease.
They create dark corners of the mind which fester.

The normal healthy mind reflects itself in a healthy body.

Happiness lies within the reach of those
who reach beyond themselves.

Great works are performed not by strength
but by perseverance.

Pride is not found in being the best but in doing your best.

If one advances confidently in the direction of his dreams,
and endeavors to live the life which he has imagined, he will
meet with a success unexpected in common hours.

When you can do the common things of life in an uncommon
way you will command the attention of the world.

Good health begins in the mind and starts with the formation
of attitudes that promote optimism, well being and enhance
the quality of life.

Yesterday I dared to struggle. Today I dared to win.

Ultimately the only power to which man should aspire,
is that which he exercises over himself.

The most successful leader of all is the one
who sees another picture not yet actualized.

Success usually comes to those who are too busy to look for it.

Conversation means being able to disagree
and still continue the discussion.

When you're making a success of something, it's not work,
it's a way of life.

Work is the greatest thing in the world.
So we should save some of it for tomorrow.

All serious daring starts from within.

Hard work spotlights the character of people:
Some turn up their sleeves, some turn up their noses,
and some don't turn up at all.

If you can't be a good example then you'll
just have to be a horrible warning.

Learn the wisdom of compromise
for it is better to bend a little than to break.

Everybody is ignorant—only on different subjects.

Plans get you into things but you have to work your way out.

If a man empties his purse into his head
no one can take it from him.

Have faith, even in darkness flowers bloom.

Sleep, riches and health to be truly enjoyed must be interrupted.

Two Days We Should Not Worry About
Yesterday: with its mistakes and heartaches.
They are gone forever.
Tomorrow: Is the other day. It has problems and possibilities,
but until the sun rises, it is unborn and unreal.
Today is the only day that matters. Only when we bear the
burdens of those other two days are we likely to fail.

You Can Bank On It

Imagine you had a bank that each morning credited your account with $1,440 — with ONE condition: whatever part of the $1,440 you failed to use during the day would be erased from your account, and no balance would be carried over. What would you do? You'd draw out EVERY cent EVERY day and use it to your best advantage.

Well, you do have such a bank, and its name is TIME. Every morning, this bank credits you with 1,440 minutes. And it writes off as forever lost whatever portion you have failed to invest to good purpose.

A Blueprint for Achievement

Believe...while others are doubting.

Plan...while others are playing.

Study...while others are sleeping.

Decide...while others are delaying.

Prepare...while others are daydreaming.

Begin...while others are wishing.

Save...while others are wasting.

Listen...while others are talking.

Smile...while others are pouting.

Commend...while others are criticizing.

Persist...while others are quitting.

Anyway

People are unreasonable, illogical and self-centered. Love them anyway. If you do good, people will accuse you of ulterior motives. Do good anyway. If you are successful, you win false friends and true enemies. Succeed anyway. The good you do today may be forgotten tomorrow. Do good anyway. Honesty and frankness make you vulnerable. Be honest and frank anyway. The biggest men and women with the biggest ideas can be shot down by the smallest minds. Think big anyway. People favor underdogs but follow only top dogs. Fight for some underdogs anyway. What you spend years building may be destroyed overnight. Build anyway. People really need help but may attack if you help them. Help people anyway. Give the world the best you have and you may get kicked in the teeth. Give the world the best you have anyway!

Live as if you liked yourself, and it may happen. Reach out, keep reaching out, keep bringing in. This is how we're going to live for a long time: for every gardener knows that after the digging, after the planting, after the long season of tending and growth, the harvest comes.

All that you do, do with all of your might. Things half done, are never done right!

Myself
—Edgar Guest

I have to live with myself and so
I want to be fit for myself to know.
I want to be able as days go by
Always to look myself straight in the eye.
I don't want to stand with the setting sun,
And hate myself for the things I've done.
I don't want to keep on a closet shelf
A lot of secrets about myself.
And fool myself as I come and go
Into thinking that nobody else will know
The kind of person I really am;
I don't want to dress myself up in sham.
I want to go out with my head erect
I want to deserve all men's respect;
But here in this struggle for fame and pelf
I want to be able to like myself.
I don't want to think as I come and go,
That I'm bluster and bluff an empty show.
I can never hide myself from me
I see what others may never see.
I know what others may never know
I never can fool myself and so —
Whatever happens I want to be
Self-respecting and conscience free.

Drinking From My Saucer

Life has had many challenges, lately and right now:
but I don't worry about that much, I'm happy anyhow.
As I go along life's journey, I'm reaping more than I sowed;
I'M DRINKING FROM MY SAUCER,
'CAUSE MY CUP HAS OVERFLOWED.

Don't have a lot of riches; so sometimes the going's rough;
but I have some friends who love me; that makes me rich
enough.
I just thank God for his blessings and the gifts that he's bestowed;
I'M DRINKING FROM MY SAUCER,
'CAUSE MY CUP HAS OVERFLOWED.

I remember times when things went wrong
and my faith got a little thin;
But sure enough, the dark clouds broke
and the sun came through again.
So God, help me not to gripe about the tough rows that I've
hoed.
I'M DRINKING FROM MY SAUCER,
'CAUSE MY CUP HAS OVERFLOWED.

So if God gives me the courage when the way gets steep and
rough
I won't ask for another blessing, I'm already blessed enough.
May I never be too busy to help another bear his load;
THEN I'LL KEEP DRINKING FROM MY SAUCER,
'CAUSE MY CUP HAS OVERFLOWED.

The Dilemma

To laugh is to risk appearing a fool.

To weep is to risk appearing sentimental.

To reach out for another is to risk involvement.

To expose feelings is to risk rejection.

To place your dreams before the crowd is to risk ridicule.

To love is to risk not being loved in return.

To go forward in the face of overwhelming odds is to risk failure.

But risks must be taken because the greatest hazard in life is to risk nothing. The person who risks nothing does nothing, has nothing, is nothing. He may avoid suffering and sorrow, but he cannot learn, feel, change, grow or love. Only a person who risks is free.

Extremes

Give me life of intense emotion.

Give me the joys of extremes.

Life with the breath and depth of the ocean.

I crave a fullness, not dreams.

Don't waste my time with a part of the story.

I want it all here and now.

Peace and slow plodding may lead to glory.

My fate is different somehow.

Let me be classed with the highest or lowest.

Only with these will my senses be keen.

You'll find me either the fastest or slowest.

I'll never rot with the dull in-between.

I Threw the Key Away

I have shut the door on yesterday.
Its sorrows and despairs.
I have locked within its gloom
Past failures and mistakes.

And now I throw the key away
and seek a sunny room
Which I will furnish with hopes and smiles
And fragrant springtime bloom.

No thought shall enter this bright room
That has a touch of pain.
No impatience, unhappiness
Shall ever entrance gain.

I shut the door on yesterday
And threw away the key.
Tomorrow holds no fear for me
Since I have found TODAY.

The clock of life is wound but once and no man has the power
To tell just when the hands will stop
On what day — or what hour.
Now is the only time you have so live it with a will.
Don't wait until tomorrow. The hands may then be still.

I invite all readers to write to us at
P.O. Box 1180, Palm Springs, CA 92263
and send any of your favorite quotations that
enabled you to reshape your mental patterns
and enhance the quality of your life by promoting
a glowing state of mental and physical health.

The end of reading is not more books —

BUT MORE LIFE!

The Institute for Phobic Awareness
Phobics Anonymous™
World Service Headquarters
P.O. Box 1180
Palm Springs, CA 92263-1180
(619) 322-COPE
Fax: (619) 416-0175

ORDER FORM

MENTAL FLOSS
_____Number of books at $9.95 each: $ _____

FROM ANXIETY ADDICT TO SERENITY SEEKER
_____Number of books at $12.95 each: $ _____

THE TWELVE STEPS OF PHOBICS ANONYMOUS
_____Number of books at $9.95 each: $ _____

California residents please add Sales Tax: $ _____

Shipping and Handling for one book: $3.00: $ 3.00
Add .50 for each additional book.
_____Additional books at .50 each= $ _____

                                    Total Enclosed $ _____

Name:_____ Tel: (_____) _____

Address: _____

City:_____ State_____ Zip _____

All checks payable to: THE INSTITUTE FOR PHOBIC AWARENESS. Foreign
International Money Orders payable in U.S. Funds. For postage outside the
U.S. add $3.00 to each book.

SPECIAL QUANTITY DISCOUNTS AVAILABLE ON REQUEST

A Non-Profit Corporation   Federal I.D. # 33-0002498   Corporate ID # 11626